Flying

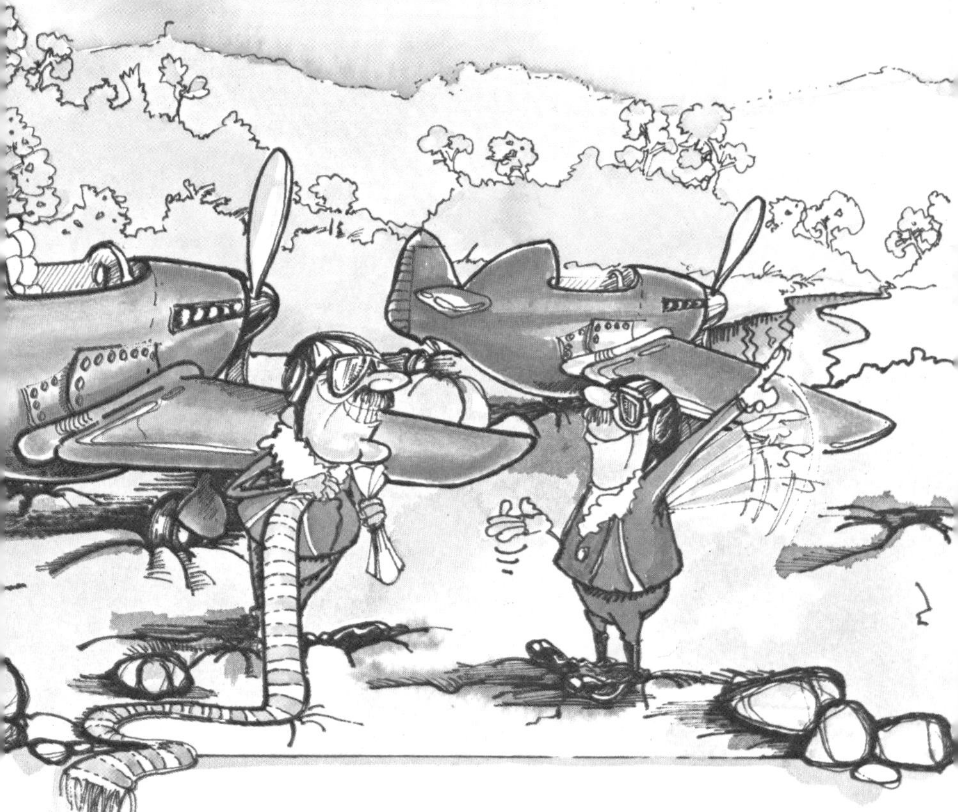

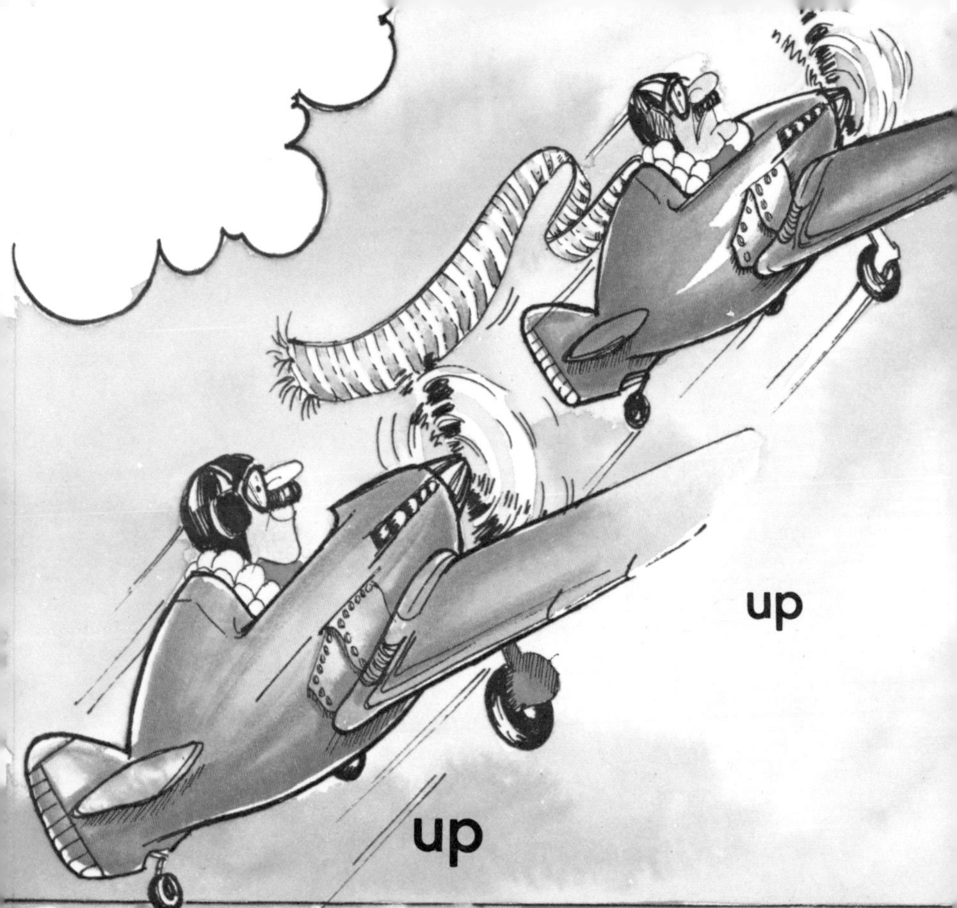

Up

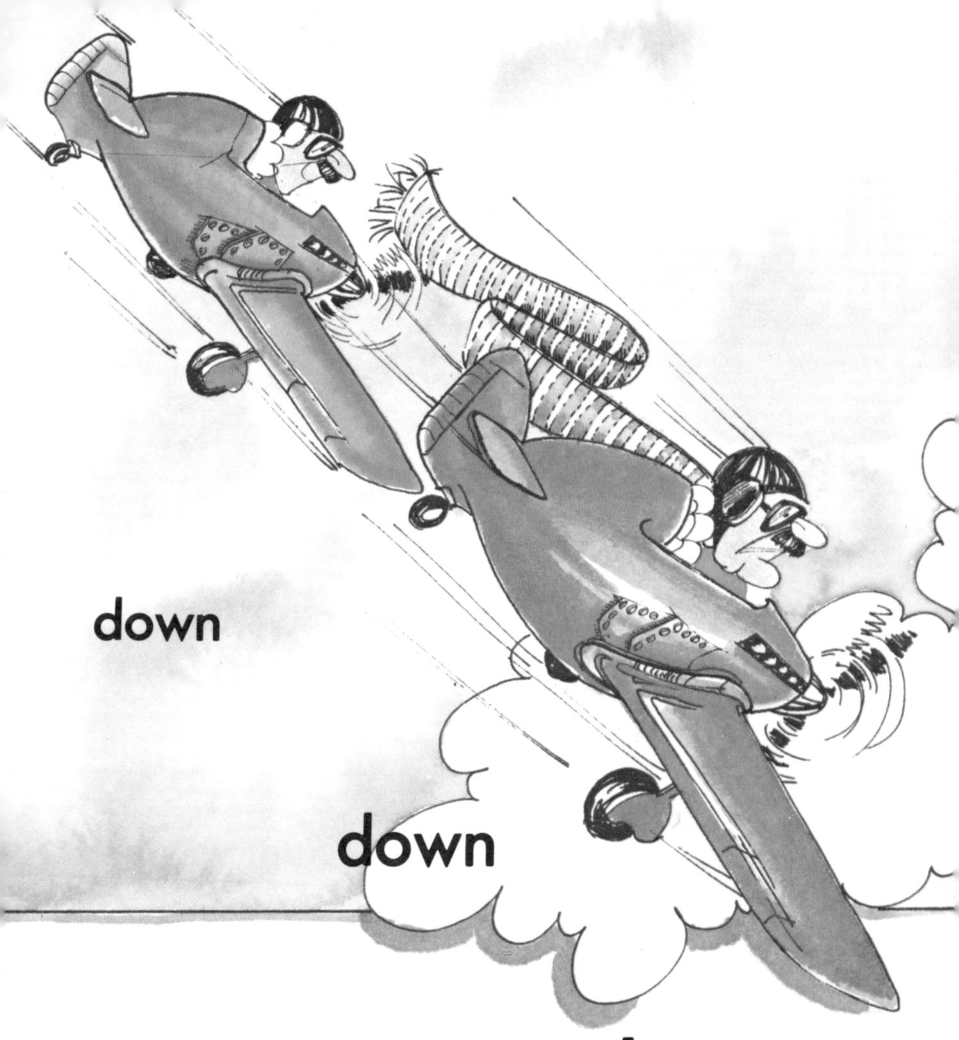

down

down

down,

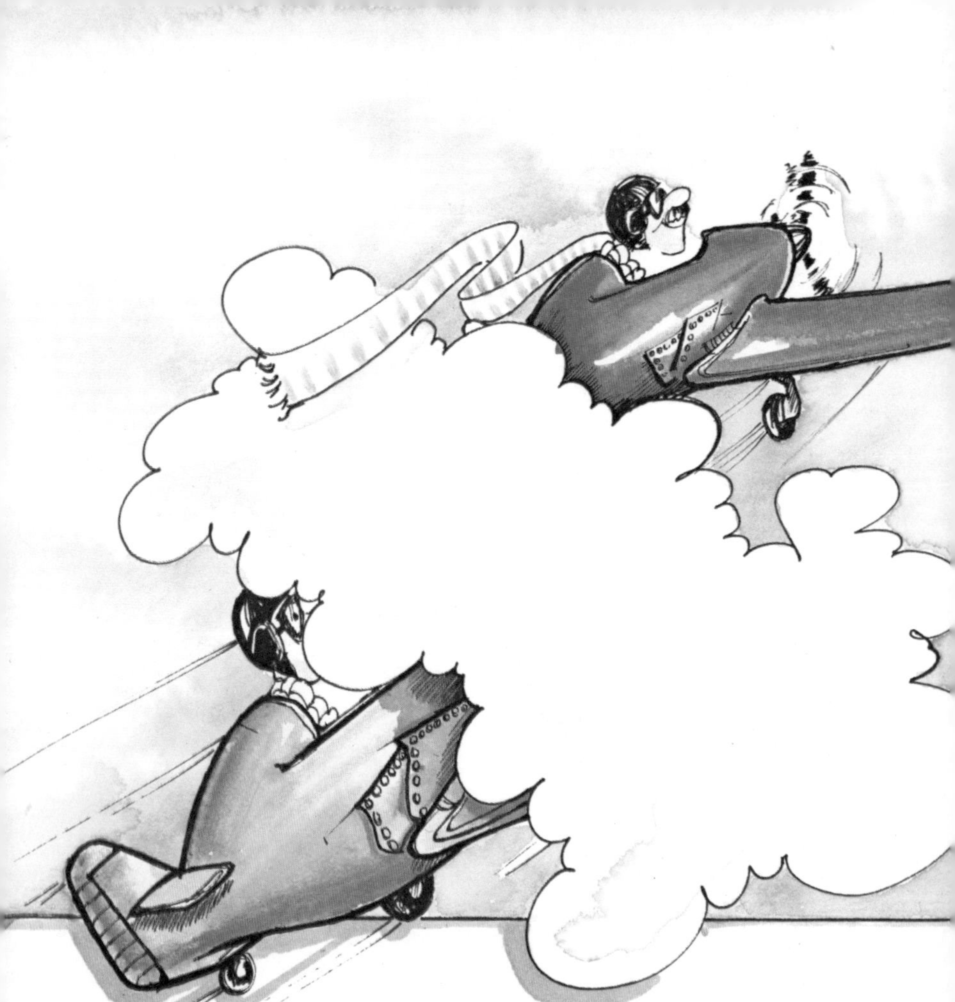

in and out,

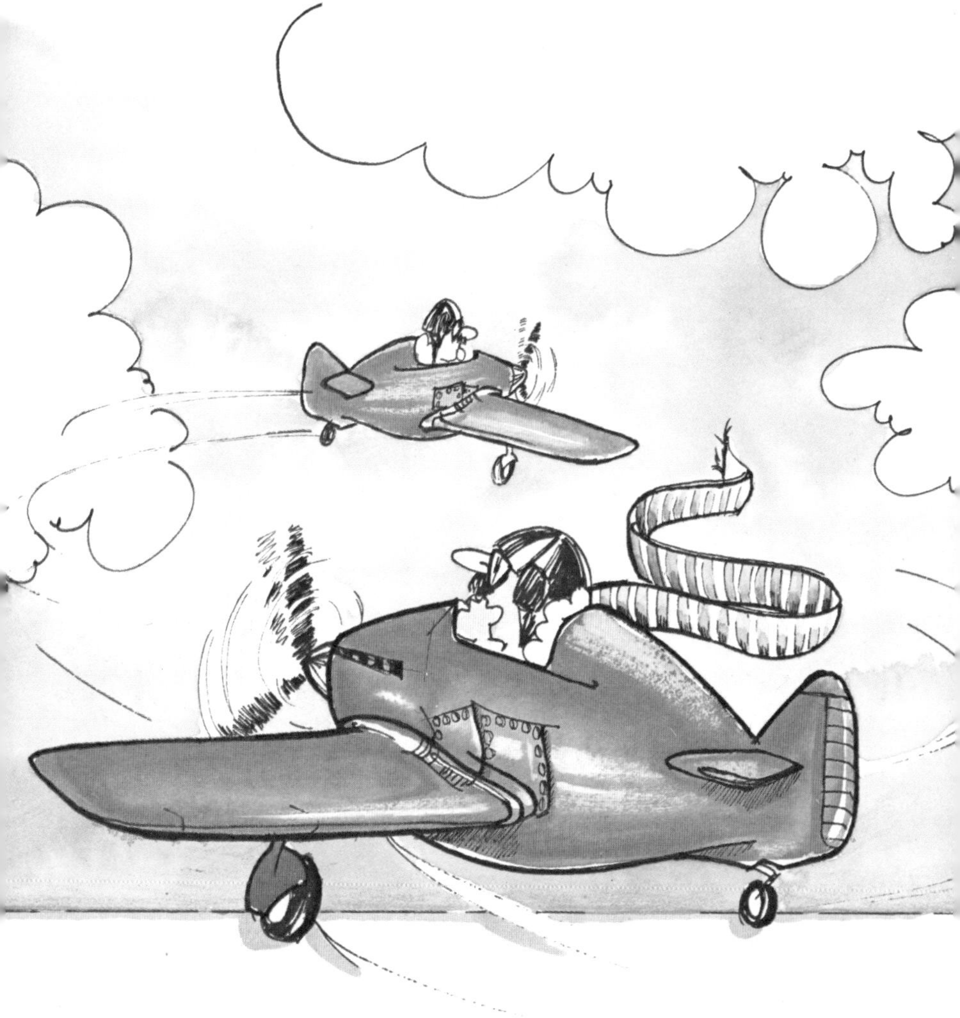

and round and round.

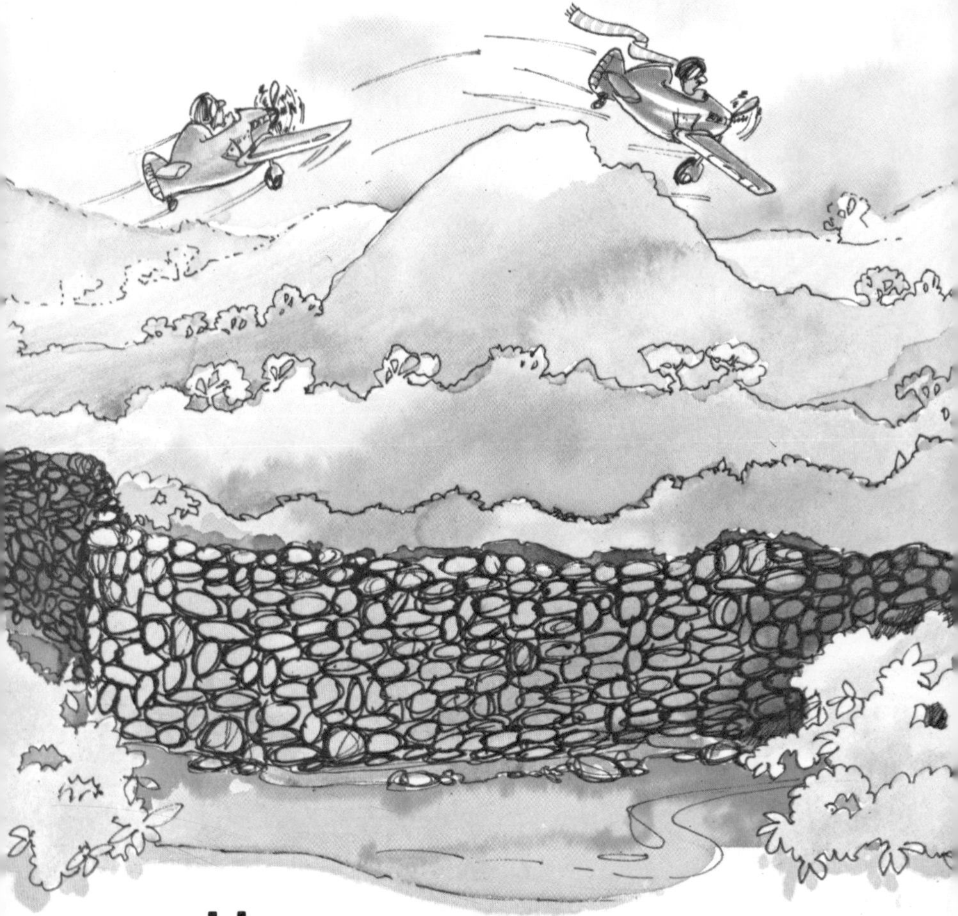

Up up up,
down down down,

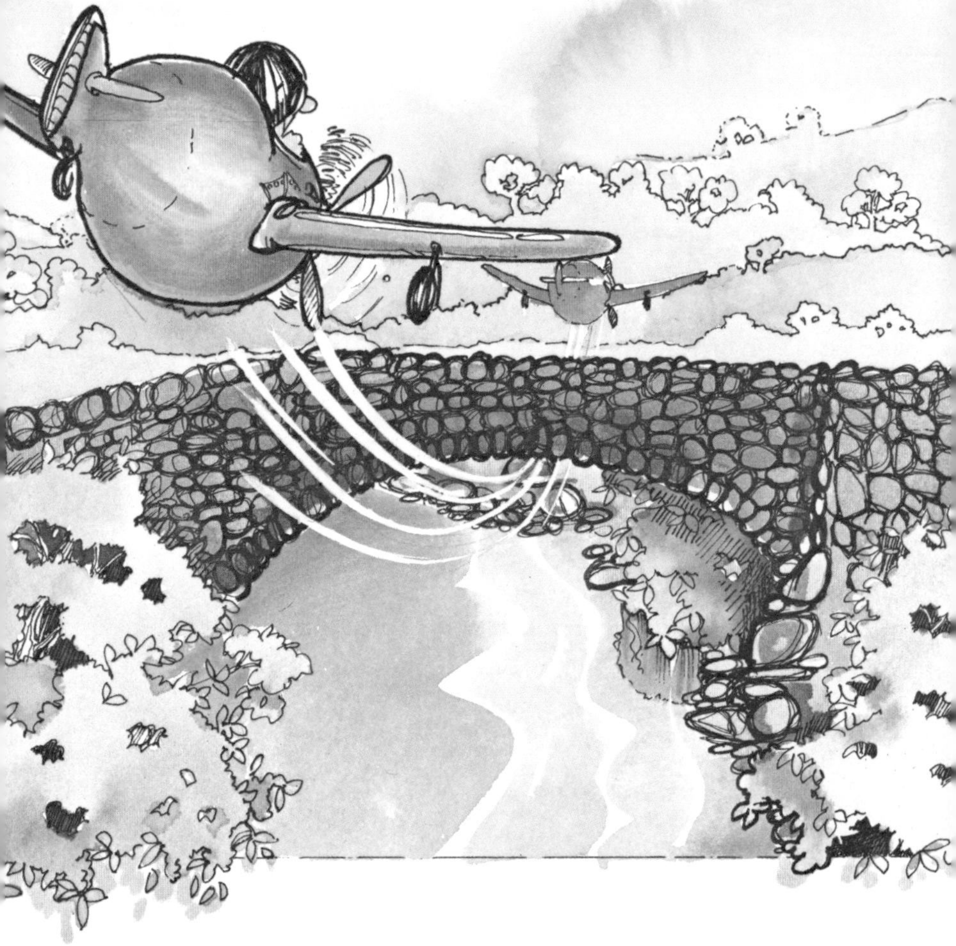

in and out,

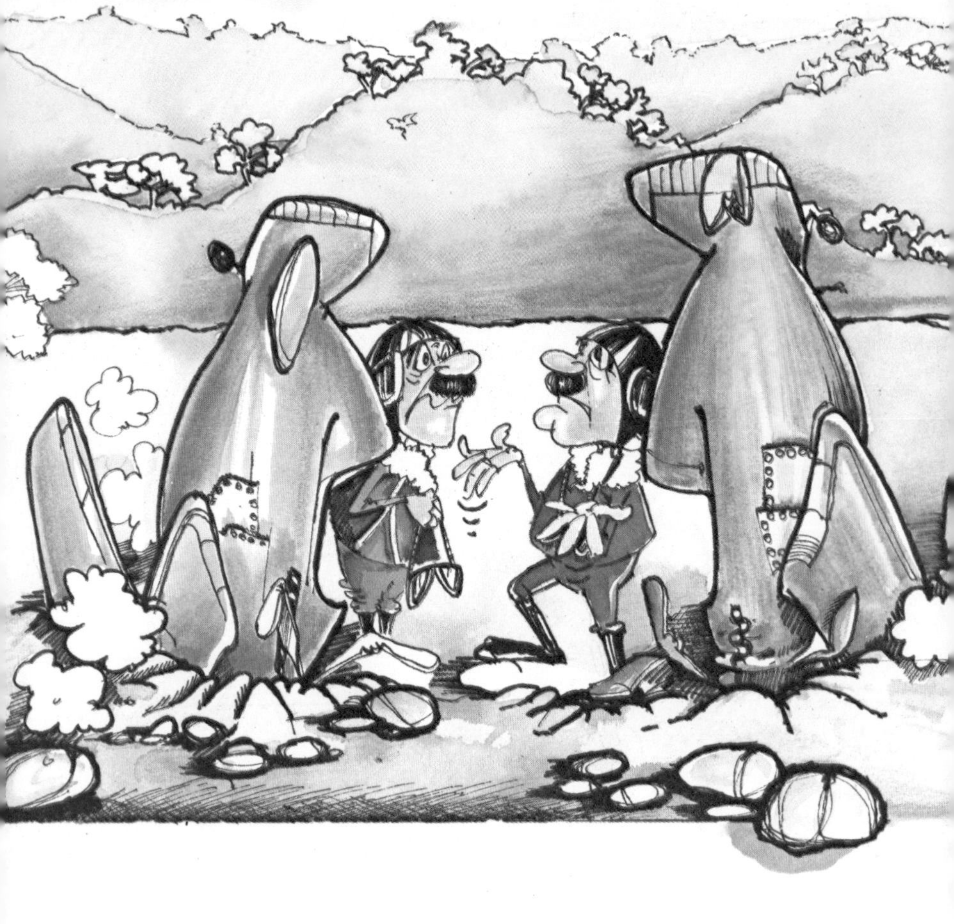

and hit the ground!